Securing Our Future: A School's Guide to ISO 27001 Certification

HELPING SCHOOLS IMPLEMENT ISO27001

"Securing Our Future" is a comprehensive guide that helps schools navigate the process of obtaining ISO 27001 certification for their information security management system (ISMS). An Information Security Management System (ISMS) is a framework consisting of policies and procedures that systematically manage an organization's sensitive data. The primary goal of an ISMS is to minimize risk and ensure business continuity by proactively limiting the impact of a security breach. It typically addresses employee behaviour and processes, as well as data and technology, and can be targeted toward specific types of data or implemented comprehensively as part of the company's culture.

The book begins with an introduction to ISO 27001, outlining its purpose, scope, and certification process. It then moves on to demonstrate how to build a strong business case for certification, identifying stakeholders, assessing the current state of information security, and presenting the benefits and costs associated with certification.

The guide highlights the importance of gaining support from the school community, including staff, students, parents, executive teams, and governing bodies. It offers strategies for communication, addressing concerns, and fostering a culture of security awareness. The book outlines assembling an implementation team, conducting a gap analysis, and developing an action plan to establish an ISMS that aligns with ISO 27001 requirements.

Furthermore, *"Securing Our Future"* discusses maintaining and continually improving the ISMS, staying current with information security trends. It emphasizes the significance of training and awareness programs for different target audiences.

Finally, it provides guidance on preparing for certification, conducting internal audits, and addressing non-conformities. The book offers insights into the certification audit process, including documentation review, on-site audit, and responding to audit findings.

Implementing a program to achieve certification in something like ISO27001 can be daunting the first time you investigate it, but the process is achievable and the benefits numerous.

Primarily, ISO 27001 embodies practical wisdom and enables you to attain the level of information security that both your organization and students rightfully deserve.

As an ISO 27001 Lead Auditor, Nick Beaugeard, the author, possesses the expertise and insight necessary to guide you through the often intricate and multifaceted world of ISO 27001 for Schools. With years of experience in the field, Beaugeard understands the unique challenges and requirements that educational institutions face in implementing and maintaining information security standards. His background in both the technical aspects of security and the educational environment ensures that he can provide tailored solutions that align with the specific needs and goals of schools. Whether you are a school administrator, IT professional, or educator looking to enhance the security of your information systems, Beaugeard's guidance can be an invaluable resource in navigating the complexities of ISO 27001, ensuring compliance, and fostering a culture of continuous improvement in information security within your educational institution.

Contents

Introduction

In today's increasingly digital world, educational institutions are faced with the complex challenge of protecting sensitive information and ensuring the privacy of their students, staff, and stakeholders. The proliferation of digital tools and platforms has revolutionized the way education is delivered, offering unprecedented opportunities for collaboration, communication, and innovation. However, this digital transformation also exposes schools to potential cybersecurity threats, ranging from data breaches to malicious attacks.

Schools must strike a delicate balance between embracing the benefits of technology and safeguarding their communities from these threats. They must implement robust security measures without stifling the creativity and flexibility that modern technology affords. This is a nuanced task that requires a comprehensive understanding of both the technological landscape and the unique needs and vulnerabilities of an educational environment.

This is where the International Organization for Standardization's ISO 27001 certification comes into play. ISO 27001 is a globally recognized standard that outlines the best practices for information security management. It provides a systematic approach to managing and protecting sensitive information using a risk management process, incorporating legal, physical, and technical controls.

For schools, obtaining ISO 27001 certification means demonstrating a commitment to the highest standards of information security. It involves implementing a structured Information Security Management System (ISMS) that aligns with the school's objectives, regulatory requirements, and the specific risks associated with its operations. This not only helps in protecting the integrity, confidentiality, and availability of data but also fosters trust among students, parents, staff, and other stakeholders.

The process of achieving ISO 27001 certification can be a rigorous one, requiring a deep understanding of the standard's requirements, a thorough assessment of existing security measures, and a commitment to continuous improvement. However, the benefits are substantial. Certification can enhance a school's reputation, provide a competitive advantage, and, most importantly, create a safer and more secure learning environment.

In an era where data breaches and cyber threats are becoming more common, the importance of information security in education cannot be overstated. By adhering to the principles and practices outlined in ISO 27001, schools can navigate the digital landscape with confidence, ensuring that they are doing everything in their power to protect the people and information that lie at the heart of their communities.

"Securing Our Future " is designed to provide schools with starting point and overview for obtaining this globally recognized certification, which serves as a testament to an institution's commitment to information security. By achieving ISO 27001 certification, schools can demonstrate to all their stakeholders, including students and their families as well as staff, the school's executive team and governing bodies, that they are

taking proactive measures to protect their community's valuable information assets.

This book begins with an overview of ISO 27001, its purpose, scope, and the certification process, helping readers to gain a solid understanding of the standard and its relevance to educational institutions. We then delve into the process of building a business case for certification, offering practical tips for assessing the current state of information security, identifying stakeholders, and presenting the benefits and costs associated with ISO 27001 certification.

To ensure the success of the certification process, we explore strategies for gaining support from the school community, fostering a culture of security awareness, and assembling an implementation team. The guide also provides a high-level overview on conducting a gap analysis, developing an action plan, and establishing an Information Security Management System (ISMS) in accordance with ISO 27001 requirements.

We address the importance of maintaining and continually improving the ISMS to ensure the ongoing effectiveness of information security measures. This includes periodic reviews, updates, staying current with information security trends, and best practices.

In addition to the technical aspects of certification, we emphasize the importance of training and awareness programs tailored for various target audiences, including staff, students, and parents. This book offers guidance on developing and delivering effective training programs and ongoing awareness initiatives that reinforce the significance of information security in the school community.

As schools progress towards certification, we discuss the process of selecting a certification body, conducting internal audits, addressing non-conformities, and making final preparations for the certification audit. We provide a look at the certification audit process, offering insights into the documentation review, on-site audit, and strategies for responding to audit findings. We recognize that obtaining ISO 27001 certification is not the end of the journey and discuss maintaining the certification.

Finally, we share our insights into applying ISO 27001 to schools and give some key points for special consideration.

By following the guidelines and recommendations provided in *"Securing Our Future* ", educational institutions will be well-prepared to navigate the certification process and create a secure environment for their communities. Through the implementation of a robust ISMS and adherence to ISO 27001 standards, schools can play a vital role in shaping a secure digital future for the generations to come.

Understanding ISO 27001

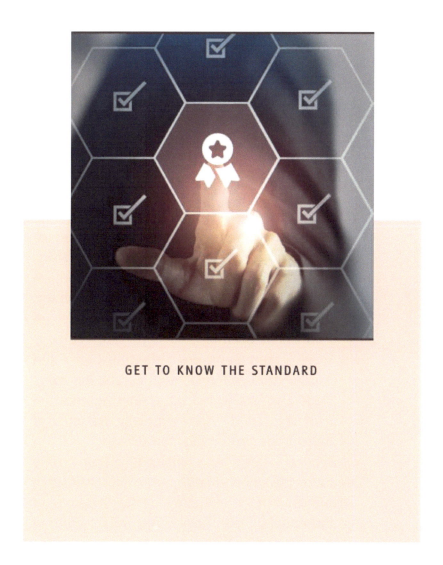

GET TO KNOW THE STANDARD

Chapter 1: Understanding ISO 27001

What is an Information Security Management System (ISMS)?

To understand the ISO 27001 standard, we must understand the ISMS that the standard refers to when setting criteria and guidelines for best practices for information security.

An Information Security Management System (ISMS) is a comprehensive set of policies, procedures, and controls designed to protect an organization's information assets. The main components of an ISMS under ISO 27001 include:

- **Policy Framework:** This includes the security policies, procedures, and guidelines that govern the overall approach to information security within the organization.
- **Risk Assessment and Management:** Identifying, evaluating, and prioritizing risks, followed by coordinated and economical application of resources to minimize, monitor, and control the probability or impact of unfortunate events.
- **Asset Management:** Identification and classification of information assets, including hardware, software, data, and intellectual property, and the implementation of appropriate protection measures.
- **Access Control:** Ensuring that only authorized individuals have access to sensitive information, including the use of authentication, authorization, and accounting mechanisms.

- **Human Resource Security:** This includes the processes for hiring, training, and managing employees to ensure that they understand and fulfill their information security responsibilities.
- **Physical and Environmental Security:** Protection of physical locations and environments where information assets are stored or accessed, including data centres, workstations, and network equipment.
- **Communications and Operations Management:** Managing the daily operations and communications, including network security, malware protection, backups, and monitoring.
- **Incident Management:** Procedures for identifying, reporting, and responding to security incidents, including breaches, vulnerabilities, and threats.
- **Business Continuity Management:** Ensuring that critical business functions continue to operate during and after a disaster or other significant disruption.
- **Compliance:** Ensuring adherence to legal, regulatory, and contractual obligations, as well as internal policies and procedures.
- **Monitoring and Improvement:** Continuous monitoring of the ISMS to ensure its effectiveness, along with regular audits and reviews to identify and implement improvements.
- **Supplier Relationships:** Managing the risks associated with third-party suppliers and

service providers, including contracts, service level agreements, and ongoing monitoring.

- **Encryption and Cryptography:** Utilizing encryption and other cryptographic controls to protect the confidentiality, integrity, and availability of information.
- **Awareness and Training:** Regular training and awareness programs to ensure that all staff members are aware of their responsibilities and the importance of information security.
- **Technology and Technical Security Controls:** Implementation of firewalls, intrusion detection systems, anti-virus software, and other technical measures to protect information assets.

What is ISO 27001?

ISO 27001 is an international standard for information security management systems (ISMS), published by the International Organization for Standardization (ISO) and the International Electrotechnical Commission (IEC). The standard provides a systematic approach to managing sensitive information by applying a risk management process and giving assurance to stakeholders that their data is protected. The creation of the enduring ISMS, and the certification to ISO:IEC 27001 is not merely a one-time checklist; rather, it is a system that ensures continuous data security. It will autonomously adjust where risk assessments pinpoint areas for enhancement or identify new threats.

Notes from the field: It's a common misconception that Schools have vastly different needs than businesses when implementing security standards. Given the range of information stored, one could argue that schools need to be more stringent. However, convincing the school community of this can be difficult. ISO 27001 helps you here as you can leverage executive sponsorship to make the needed changes, for example in password policy.

The purpose and scope of ISO 27001

The primary purpose of ISO 27001 is to help organizations of all sizes and industries establish, implement, maintain, and improve an ISMS. The scope of the standard covers all forms of information, whether digital, paper-based, or otherwise. The ISMS serves as a framework for identifying, assessing, and managing information security risks while ensuring the confidentiality, integrity, and availability of information assets.

Notes from the field: Educating the school about ISO 27001 is important to ensure that stakeholders understand the ramifications of what you are doing. Use the content in this book to help your stakeholders get on board early.

The certification process

The ISO 27001 certification process involves several key steps, which include:

1. **Establishing an ISMS:** The organization must create an ISMS based on the requirements of the ISO 27001 standard.

2. **Conducting a risk assessment:** The organization must identify and evaluate the information security risks relevant to its operations.
3. **Implementing security controls:** The organization must select and apply appropriate security controls from ISO 27001 Annex A or other sources to mitigate the identified risks.
4. **Conducting internal audits and management reviews:** The organization must regularly review the ISMS to ensure its continued effectiveness and compliance with the standard.
5. **Selecting a certification body:** The organization must choose an accredited certification body to conduct the external audit and validate its compliance with ISO 27001.
6. **Certification audit:** The certification body conducts a two-stage audit, including a documentation review and an on-site assessment of the organization's ISMS.
7. **Certification:** If the audit is successful, the organization is awarded an ISO 27001 certificate, valid for three years

The why

ISO 27001 certification for a school can be a strategic decision that brings several benefits. Here's why a school might pursue this certification:

1. **Data Protection**: Schools handle a significant amount of sensitive data, including student records, staff information, financial details, and more. ISO 27001 helps in implementing robust security measures to protect this data.
2. **Regulatory Compliance**: Depending on the jurisdiction, there may be legal and regulatory

requirements related to data protection that schools must comply with. ISO 27001 certification can demonstrate compliance with these regulations.

3. **Reputation Enhancement**: Achieving ISO 27001 certification can enhance the reputation of the school by demonstrating a commitment to information security. It can be a strong selling point to parents, students, and staff.

4. **Risk Management**: The standard helps in identifying, assessing, and managing information security risks, ensuring that the school is prepared to deal with potential threats and vulnerabilities.

5. **Operational Improvement**: Implementing the ISMS according to ISO 27001 can lead to more efficient and effective processes within the school, improving overall operations.

6. **Third-Party Relationships**: If the school works with third-party vendors or partners, having ISO 27001 certification can provide assurance regarding the security of shared information.

7. **Building Trust**: Parents, students, and staff can have increased confidence in the school's ability to protect personal and sensitive information, building trust within the community.

8. **Cybersecurity Education**: The process of achieving certification can also be an educational opportunity, raising awareness about cybersecurity among students and staff.

9. **Insurance Benefits**: Some insurance providers may offer better terms or premiums to organizations that have demonstrated a

commitment to security through ISO 27001 certification.

10. **Alignment with Other Standards**: ISO 27001 can be integrated with other management standards that the school might be following, creating a cohesive management system.

11. **Disaster Recovery**: The standard includes provisions for business continuity and disaster recovery planning, ensuring that the school can continue to function in the event of an incident.

12. **Competitive Advantage**: If the school is in a competitive environment, ISO 27001 certification can be a differentiator, attracting more students and quality staff.

In conclusion, ISO 27001 certification for a school is not just about compliance: it's about creating a culture of security, improving operations, building trust, and enhancing the reputation of the institution. It reflects a proactive approach to managing information security risks and can be a valuable asset for any educational institution.

BUILDING THE
BUSINESS CASE

MAKING THE RIGHT
DECISIONS

Chapter 2: Building the Business Case

Most ISO 27001 projects don't get started without a business case. It is important to have this in place before you start to ensure the appropriate level of funding and executive sponsorship to complete the project properly. This chapter discusses the business case and what you may need to do to complete it.

Identifying the stakeholders

Before embarking on the ISO 27001 certification journey, it is crucial to identify the stakeholders who will be involved in or affected by the implementation process. Stakeholders may include staff, students, parents, executive teams, governing bodies, and external partners. Understanding their needs, expectations, and concerns will help shape the business case and communication strategy for the certification process. Chapter 3 delves deeper into the subject of communication and securing support from stakeholders within the school.

> **Notes from the field:** Having a diverse range of stakeholders is critical, as is the need to engage them early. Some stakeholders will be surprised that you are doing this now, assuming it was already done. This expectation reset can cause conflict, so make sure you engineer buy-in from the top down.

A meticulous identification of stakeholders can aid in making sure that all essential areas are represented when assembling your implementation team, as detailed in Chapter 4.

Benefits of ISO 27001 certification for schools

To build a compelling business case, highlight the benefits of ISO 27001 certification for schools, such as:

- **Enhanced reputation and competitive advantage**: ISO 27001 certification can differentiate a high school from competitors. Certification demonstrates a school's commitment to information security, instilling trust and confidence among stakeholders. This in turn can lead to increased enrolments and potential school expansion if the school has the capacity to accommodate these.
- **Regulatory compliance**: Compliance with an internationally recognized standard may help meet legal and regulatory requirements related to data protection. This may reduce overhead costs in other school governance areas.
- **Improved risk management**: The implementation of an ISMS ensures that potential risks are identified, assessed and managed proactively.
- **Avoiding costs and pitfalls associated with the realization of risks**: This includes reputational damage being avoided, as could occur if there was a significant data breach. A look at organizations that have had public security breaches of different kinds, would provide an indication of the kind of monetary and reputational losses that the school would rather avoid and can help build a financial case for proceeding with ISO 27001 certification.
- **Greater operational efficiency**: A well-defined ISMS streamlines processes, reduces duplication of efforts, and increases overall efficiency. In

putting forward your business case, try to identify where these efficiencies equate to cost savings.

Notes from the field: For independent schools, announcing the start of this process to the parent community can commonly bring assistance from parents. Many schools will find parents who have already achieved this certification in their roles within the commercial world.

However, be clear with the messaging as some of these topics are complex and may confuse some in the parent community. Ensure your teams are ready and prepared to discuss and clarify questions on this. You may also take the choice of only announcing on completion of certification.

Costs and resource requirements

To present a comprehensive business case, it is essential to outline the costs and resource requirements associated with ISO 27001 certification. These may include:

1. **Initial implementation costs**: Costs for updating policies, procedures, and controls, as well as any required investments in technology or infrastructure. Also, any expenditure on third party consulting or software to assist in the implementation process if the school does not want to manage the process solely with in house resources.
2. **Training and awareness programs**: Expenses related to developing and delivering training and awareness initiatives for staff, students, and parents.

3. **Certification fees**: Fees charged by the certification body for conducting the certification audit.
4. **Ongoing maintenance costs**: Expenses associated with maintaining and improving the ISMS, including periodic internal audits, management reviews, and recertification audits.

Notes from the field: Schools should estimate an overall budget (including external consulting, certification, and external audits) of the equivalent of a fully loaded staff member's cost per year to achieve certification and then about 25% of a fully loaded staff member's equivalent cost each year following to maintain and improve.

Assessing the current state of information security

An initial assessment of the school's current information security practices is essential to establish a baseline for improvement.

It may be helpful in gaining stakeholder buy-in to assess the current status of information security prior to presenting your business case. This will require some resource allocation which may or may not be available before project approval and may not be helpful in all cases.

This assessment should involve reviewing existing policies, procedures, and controls, as well as identifying potential vulnerabilities and gaps. This can provide a clearer understanding of the resources and efforts required to achieve ISO 27001 certification.

Notes from the field: Most organizations are shocked and surprised at the initial level of information security. This is perfectly normal. You're doing ISO27001 to fix that.

An alternative method consists of operating under the assumption that nothing meets the standard, and you are beginning from the ground up. Pointing out specific gaps and vulnerabilities to stakeholders might be perceived as using fear tactics, and this approach may negatively impact those you need to persuade.

Skipping any gap analysis and assuming total non-compliance is a perfectly acceptable approach in some scenarios, especially when starting an information security management system (ISMS) from scratch. By assuming that no existing controls or processes meet the required standards, the organization can approach the implementation with a clean slate, ensuring that every aspect is designed and aligned with the specific requirements of the standard. This approach might be the most appropriate way to achieve certification in cases where existing systems are outdated, fragmented, or where there is a lack of confidence in current compliance levels. It allows for a comprehensive and cohesive development of the ISMS, without the potential biases or constraints of existing practices. This method can foster a culture of thoroughness and excellence, focusing on building a robust system that not only meets but exceeds the standard's requirements, rather than merely patching up existing weaknesses. It ensures that nothing is overlooked, and every element is tailored to the organization's unique needs and risks.

Presenting the business case to stakeholders

Once the benefits, costs, and resource requirements have been identified, it is crucial to present a well-structured business case to the relevant stakeholders. This presentation should emphasize the value of ISO 27001 certification in enhancing the school's reputation, improving risk management, and ensuring the protection of sensitive information. It should also address any concerns or objections that stakeholders may have, providing clear explanations and evidence to support the certification initiative. Tailor the presentation to each stakeholder group, focusing on the specific benefits that are most relevant to their needs and interests.

When presenting the business case:

- Clearly articulate the objectives and scope of the ISO 27001 certification project.
- Emphasize the long-term benefits of certification, both tangible and intangible.
- Where possible, compare the costs of implementation with the savings that can be measured, and the avoidance of costs associated with risks being realised.
- Provide a realistic timeline for implementation, highlighting key milestones and deliverables.
- Address potential risks and challenges, along with strategies for overcoming them.
- Demonstrate the school's commitment to information security and the well-being of its community.

By presenting a well-reasoned, evidence-based business case for ISO 27001 certification, you can garner the support of stakeholders and set the stage for a successful implementation process.

Chapter 3: Gaining Support from the School Community

Communicating the importance of information security

Effectively communicating the importance of information security to the school community is critical for gaining support and fostering a culture of security awareness. Develop a communication plan that highlights the relevance of information security to the school's mission and values, and underscores the risks associated with inadequate security measures. Use various communication channels, such as staff meetings, parent-teacher conferences, newsletters, and social media, to reach different stakeholder groups.

Notes from the field: Skills and interest in technology vary widely in the school community. Ensure your communication plan is simple enough for all faculty and staff members to readily understand. Failure to do this will, at best, result in confusion and at worst members of staff working against the project.

Addressing concerns and objections

It is natural for stakeholders to have concerns or objections about the ISO 27001 certification process. To address these concerns, listen actively, provide clear and accurate information, and emphasize the benefits of certification. Common concerns may include costs, resource allocation, potential disruptions, and the complexity of the process. Provide reassurance by presenting a well-structured plan, offering examples of successful implementations in other schools, and highlighting the long-term value of certification.

Demonstrating the benefits of ISO 27001 certification

To gain support from stakeholders, it is essential to demonstrate the tangible and intangible benefits of ISO 27001 certification. Share success stories from other schools or organizations that have achieved certification, highlighting improvements in risk management, operational efficiency, and stakeholder trust. Additionally, provide concrete examples of how the certification process can lead to a safer and more secure learning environment for students, staff, and parents.

Creating a culture of security awareness

A strong culture of security awareness is vital for the successful implementation and maintenance of an ISMS. Encourage a sense of shared responsibility for information security among all members of the school community. Develop training and awareness programs tailored to the needs of different stakeholder groups, emphasizing the role that each individual plays in protecting the school's information assets. Regularly share updates on the progress of the ISO 27001 certification process, celebrate milestones, and acknowledge the contributions of individuals and teams in fostering a secure environment.

Summary

By effectively communicating the importance of information security, addressing concerns, demonstrating the benefits of certification, and creating a culture of security awareness, you can garner the support of the school community and pave the way for a successful ISO 27001 certification journey.

ASSEMBLING THE
IMPLEMENTATION TEAM

READY TO GET TO WORK!

Chapter 4: Assembling the Implementation Team

Implementation Team

The first step in the ISO 27001 certification process is to assemble a dedicated implementation team. This team should consist of individuals with diverse expertise and backgrounds, including representatives from IT, administration, faculty, and other relevant departments. The work previously done in identifying stakeholders should help determine who needs to be involved. The team should be led by a project manager who has experience in information security and project management, ensuring effective coordination and progress tracking.

Scope

At this point, it is good practice to define the scope of the school's sensitive data and therefore the scope of the ISMS. Most schools deal with external bodies and third-party software for example. The team needs to decide which situations involve potential sharing or exposure of the sensitive information of the school and their stakeholders. The scope needs to be determined to include or exclude these external influences depending on the way they interface with the school. If external providers are included in the scope, additional roles may be required in the implementation team to work with outside agencies.

Defining roles and responsibilities

Clearly define the roles and responsibilities of each team member to ensure a smooth and efficient implementation process. Key roles may include:

- **Project Manager**: Oversees the certification project, manages resources, and coordinates activities.
- **Information Security Officer**: Develops and maintains the ISMS, ensuring compliance with ISO 27001 requirements.
- **Risk Manager**: Identifies and assesses information security risks and oversees risk treatment activities.
- **Technical Team**: Implements and maintains security controls and technologies.
- **Training Coordinator**: Develops and delivers training and awareness programs for staff, students, and parents.
- **Other stakeholder team members** who do not have technical backgrounds may be involved in communicating back to their cohort and ensuring that any concerns raised are communicated to the team.

Conducting a gap analysis

As discussed in Chapter 2, under "Assessing the current state of information security", a gap analysis is a systematic assessment of the school's current information security practices against the requirements of ISO 27001. The purpose of the gap analysis is to identify areas of non-compliance and develop an action plan to address these gaps. If this was not performed as part of providing a business case for proceeding with ISO 27001 certification, the implementation team should review the school's existing policies, procedures, and controls, comparing them with the ISO 27001 standard.

Prioritizing gaps and developing an action plan

Once the gap analysis is complete, prioritize the identified gaps based on their impact on the school's information security and the resources required to address them. Develop a comprehensive action plan that outlines the steps needed to close these gaps, including:

- **Updating or creating new policies and procedures**: This may involve revising existing guidelines or formulating entirely new ones to align with the standards.
- **Implementing or enhancing security controls**: This includes strengthening existing security measures or introducing new ones to safeguard information.
- **Conducting risk assessments and risk treatment activities**: Regularly evaluating and mitigating risks ensures that the school's information security remains robust.
- **Developing and delivering training and awareness programs**: Educating staff and students about security protocols is vital for maintaining a secure environment.
- **Upgrading software and hardware**: Achieving compliance may necessitate updating or replacing outdated software and hardware. This ensures that the school's technology environment meets current security standards and can effectively mitigate potential threats.

The action plan should include specific tasks, responsibilities, deadlines, and resource requirements, ensuring that the implementation team can effectively monitor progress and make adjustments as needed. By considering all these aspects, the school can create a cohesive and comprehensive approach to information security, aligning with best practices and achieving certification. This not only enhances the security posture but also fosters a culture of continuous improvement and adaptability within the school's information security management system.

Summary

By assembling a dedicated implementation team, conducting a gap analysis, and developing a targeted action plan, schools can lay a strong foundation for the successful implementation of an ISMS and progress towards ISO 27001 certification.

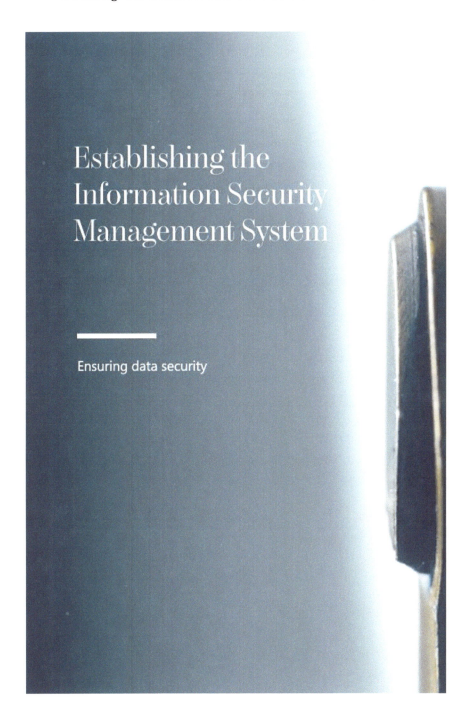

Establishing the Information Security Management System

Ensuring data security

Chapter 5: Establishing the Information Security Management System (ISMS)

Support from the top

It is critical for success that the school leadership team supports and sponsors the ISO 27001 certification process. It is important that no overall school policies or mission statements conflict with information security objectives. Likewise, the information security policies and procedures created to meet ISO 27001 requirements need to fit in with the overall direction of school policies and mission statements while not compromising the criteria required to meet ISO 27001.

Furthermore, the ISMS implementation team cannot be an island separate to the school ICT (Information and Communications Technology) department. Overall mission and direction statements for the ICT department need to be reviewed (or created) to meet the level of diligence to information security that is needed for ISO 27001 certification. The ISMS will need to be integrated into the normal workings of the ICT department, so buy-in from department leaders is essential. ICT leaders need to ensure cooperation of their resources and be ready to smooth over situations where necessary change may be resisted within the department.

Developing information security policies

The foundation of an ISMS is a set of clear and comprehensive information security policies. These policies should align with the school's mission, objectives, and risk appetite, and provide guidance on the management and protection of information assets. Key policy areas to address include:

1. **Information Security Policy**:
   a. Definition of the organization's information security objectives.
   b. Alignment with business strategy and regulatory requirements.
   c. Regular review and updates to the policy.
2. **Organization of Information Security:**
   a. Definition of roles and responsibilities.
   b. Segregation of duties.
   c. Contact with authorities and special interest groups.
3. **Human Resource Security:**
   a. Security responsibilities defined in job descriptions.
   b. Security awareness, education, and training.
   c. Disciplinary process for security violations.
4. **Asset Management:**
   a. Inventory of assets.
   b. Classification and handling of information.
   c. Acceptable use of assets.
5. **Access Control:**
   a. User access management.
   b. User responsibilities for safeguarding credentials.
   c. Clear desk and clear screen policy.
6. **Cryptography:**
   a. Encryption and key management.
   b. Policy on the use of cryptographic controls.
7. **Physical and Environmental Security:**
   a. Secure areas.
   b. Equipment security.

    c. Protection against threats from natural disasters, malicious attack, or accidents.

8. **Operations Security:**
   a. Operational procedures and responsibilities.
   b. Protection from malware.
   c. Backup and logging.

9. **Communications Security:**
   a. Network security management.
   b. Information transfer policies and procedures.

10. **System Acquisition, Development, and Maintenance:**
    a. Security requirements for information systems.
    b. Secure development environment.
    c. System change control procedures.

11. **Supplier Relationships:**
    a. Information security in supplier agreements.
    b. Supplier service delivery management.

12. **Incident Management:**
    a. Reporting information security events and weaknesses.
    b. Response and management of information security incidents.

13. **Business Continuity Management:**
    a. Information security aspects of business continuity planning.
    b. Redundancies and failover strategies.

14. **Compliance:**
    a. Identification of applicable laws and regulations.
    b. Intellectual property rights.

       c. Protection of records and privacy.

15. **Risk Management:**
    a. Risk assessment and risk treatment.
    b. Regular review and update of the risk assessment.

16. **Monitoring, Measurement, Analysis, and Evaluation:**
    a. Regular audits and assessments.
    b. Continuous improvement of the ISMS.

17. **Documentation:**
    a. Documented information required by the standard.
    b. Control of documented information.

These areas are aligned with the clauses and controls of the ISO 27001 standard and are essential for the development, implementation, and continuous improvement of an ISMS. Ensure that policies are approved by the executive team and regularly reviewed and updated to reflect changes in the school's environment and risk landscape.

Implementing security controls

In the realm of information security, a security control serves as a gauge to enhance or sustain a particular security risk. These controls are vital components in the overall security architecture and are instrumental in safeguarding information assets. ISO 27001 provides an extensive yet generic list of suggested controls in Annex A of the standard. These controls are also replicated at the end of this book for easy reference.

Implementing security controls is a multifaceted process that can be approached in various ways, depending on the specific needs, risks, and objectives of the organization. The controls may encompass:

1. **Technical Measures**: These include technological solutions designed to protect against cyber threats. Examples of technical measures are firewalls, which act as barriers to unauthorized access; encryption, which secures data by converting it into a code; antivirus software, which detects and removes malicious programs; and intrusion detection systems, which monitor and alert on suspicious activities.

2. **Administrative Controls**: These are the policies, procedures, and guidelines that govern the way an organization manages and protects its information. Administrative controls might include training programs to educate staff about security best practices, incident response plans to ensure a coordinated reaction to security breaches, access control policies to restrict who can access certain information, and regular audits to assess compliance with security policies.

3. **Physical Controls**: These are measures taken to protect the physical infrastructure where information is stored or processed. This might include secure access to data centres, surveillance cameras, secure disposal of sensitive information, and environmental controls like fire suppression systems.

4. **Human Factors**: Recognizing that people are often the weakest link in security, controls may also focus on human behaviour. This could involve ongoing awareness campaigns, regular security training, clear communication of security policies,

and fostering a culture of security within the organization.

5. **Compliance and Legal Considerations**: Ensuring that all security controls are in line with legal, regulatory, and contractual obligations is crucial. This might involve regular reviews and updates to ensure that controls meet current legal requirements.

6. **Risk-Based Approach**: Implementing security controls should be aligned with the organization's risk assessment and risk management processes. This ensures that controls are targeted at the most significant risks and that resources are used effectively.

7. **Continuous Monitoring and Improvement**: Security is a dynamic field, and threats evolve constantly. Continuous monitoring of controls and regular reviews and updates are essential to ensure that they remain effective in the changing threat landscape.

The school needs to decide which of the controls they will implement and needs to justify why they would not implement a control. Also, if the school has requirements not covered by the listed controls, they may add controls of their own.

It is good practice to use risk assessment and a risk treatment plan to select the appropriate security controls to mitigate the risks identified and to implement any required treatment of them. The resulting set of controls should be checked against the set provided in ISO 27001 Annex A for completeness.

Ensure that controls are proportionate to the level of risk and that their effectiveness is periodically assessed and adjusted as needed.

Conducting risk assessments

Risk assessments are an essential part of an ISMS, helping to identify and evaluate potential threats to information assets. Develop a risk assessment methodology that aligns with the school's risk appetite and the ISO 27001 standard. There should be a process to regularly conduct risk assessments to identify new risks and reassess existing risks, updating the risk treatment plan accordingly. It is also a good idea to perform additional risk assessments when there are major changes occurring in school systems, such as switching to new software. Changes to the way things are done may create new security risks requiring treatment and a well-timed risk assessment can help identify these. Ensure that risk assessments are documented and communicated to relevant stakeholders.

When conducting a risk assessment, the following framework may be useful:

1. **Identify the Scope**
   a. **What**: Define what areas, systems, and information will be included in the risk assessment.
   b. **Who**: Involve school administrators, IT staff, legal advisors, and possibly representatives from the student body and parents.
2. **Identify Assets and Resources**
   a. **What**: List all assets that need protection, including student records, staff

information, financial data, hardware, software, etc.

   b. **Who**: IT department, administrative staff, and department heads.

3. **Identify Threats and Vulnerabilities**

   a. **What**: Identify potential threats (e.g., cyberattacks, human error) and vulnerabilities (e.g., outdated software, weak passwords).

   b. **Who**: IT professionals, security consultants, and staff responsible for various school functions.

4. **Assess Potential Impact and Likelihood**

   a. **What**: Evaluate the potential impact of each identified risk on the school's operations, reputation, legal compliance, etc., and the likelihood of occurrence.

   b. **Who**: School leadership, IT experts, legal advisors, and other relevant stakeholders.

5. **Determine Risk Levels**

   a. **What**: Rank the risks based on their potential impact and likelihood, categorizing them as low, medium, or high.

   b. **Who**: Risk management team, including school administrators, IT staff, and possibly external consultants.

6. **Develop Mitigation Strategies**

   a. **What**: Propose measures to mitigate or eliminate the identified risks, considering cost, feasibility, and effectiveness.

   b. **Who**: IT department, school leadership, legal advisors, and other relevant experts.

7. **Document the Findings**

a. **What**: Create a comprehensive risk assessment report detailing the findings, risk levels, and recommended mitigation strategies.

b. **Output**: The output should be a formal document that serves as a guide for implementing security controls and is a reference for future assessments.

c. **Who**: Risk assessment team, with input from all involved stakeholders.

8. **Review and Update Regularly**

a. **What**: Regularly review and update the risk assessment to reflect changes in the school's environment, technology, regulations, etc.

b. **Who**: Ongoing responsibility of the school's risk management team, with periodic external audits if necessary.

Risk treatment plan

A Risk Treatment Plan is a critical step in the information security management process, particularly following a comprehensive risk assessment. It outlines the strategies and actions to mitigate unacceptable risks and maintain those at acceptable levels. Here is an expanded guide on formulating a Risk Treatment Plan:

1. **Utilize Risk Assessment Outcome**

a. **What**: Start with the findings from the risk assessment, focusing on the identified risks, their categorization, and the potential impact and likelihood.

b. **Who**: Risk management team, IT professionals, school administrators, and other stakeholders involved in the risk assessment.

2. **Define Appropriate Treatments**
   a. **What:** Determine the treatments or security controls suitable for mitigating the identified risks. These may include preventive, detective, corrective, or compensatory measures.
   b. **Who**: Security experts, IT staff, legal advisors, and school leadership.

3. **Refer to Standard Guidelines**
   a. **What**: Check against Annex A of the ISO 27001 standard (or relevant standard) to ensure that all relevant controls have been considered.
   b. **Who**: Compliance officers, IT professionals, and external consultants if needed.

4. **Document Inclusion and Omission of Controls**
   a. **What**: If any controls are to be omitted, the reasoning should be documented. Likewise, the rationale for included controls should be documented, along with their implementation status.
   b. **Who**: Risk management team, in collaboration with IT and legal advisors.

5. **Formulate an Implementation Plan**
   a. **What**: Develop a detailed plan to bring the implementation of controls to the required level. This should include specific actions, timelines, responsibilities, resources, and monitoring mechanisms.

    b. **Who**: Project managers, IT staff, school administrators, and other relevant stakeholders.

6. **Agree on Acceptable Risk Exposure**
   a. **What**: Define what constitutes an acceptable level of risk exposure, considering the school's risk appetite, legal requirements, and stakeholder expectations.
   b. **Who**: School leadership, risk management team, legal advisors, and possibly representatives from the student body and parents.

7. **Monitor and Review**
   a. **What**: Implement regular monitoring and review processes to ensure that the risk treatment plan is effectively executed and remains aligned with the school's evolving needs and environment.
   b. **Who**: Ongoing responsibility of the risk management team, with periodic external audits if necessary.

8. **Maintain Documentation**
   a. **What**: Keep all documentation up to date, including the risk treatment plan, implementation status, decisions regarding controls, and any changes or updates.
   b. **Who**: Compliance officers, risk management team, and IT staff.

A Risk Treatment Plan is a dynamic and collaborative document that translates the outcomes of a risk assessment into actionable strategies for managing information security risks. In the context of high schools, it requires careful consideration of the unique environment, stakeholders, legal obligations, and the specific risks identified. By aligning with standard guidelines like ISO 27001 and maintaining clear documentation, schools can ensure that their Risk Treatment Plan is robust, compliant, and effective in safeguarding the integrity, confidentiality, and availability of information. It represents a commitment to proactive risk management and contributes to building a resilient and secure information security posture.

Monitoring and measuring the ISMS

Ensuring the ongoing effectiveness of the Information Security Management System (ISMS) is vital for any organization, including high schools. A robust framework for monitoring and measuring its performance is essential to align with the school's information security objectives and the ISO 27001 standard. Here's a guide:

1. **Establish a Monitoring Framework**
   a. **What**: Create a structured framework that outlines how the ISMS will be monitored, including methodologies, tools, frequency, and responsibilities.
   b. **Who**: ISMS management team, IT professionals, school administrators, and possibly external consultants.
2. **Define Key Performance Indicators (KPIs)**
   a. **What**: Identify specific KPIs that reflect the school's information security objectives. These might include metrics related to incident response times, user compliance rates, system uptime, etc.

    b. **Who**: Security experts, IT staff, school leadership, and other relevant stakeholders.

3. **Regular Data Collection and Analysis**
   a. **What**: Implement processes for regularly collecting and analysing performance data. This involves gathering information from various sources like logs, surveys, audits, and more.
   b. **Who**: Designated staff responsible for monitoring, such as IT personnel, compliance officers, or a dedicated monitoring team.

4. **Identify Trends and Assess Effectiveness**
   a. **What**: Use the collected data to identify trends, assess the effectiveness of controls, and evaluate the overall performance of the ISMS.
   b. **Who**: Analysts, IT professionals, and the ISMS management team.

5. **Guide Continuous Improvement Efforts**
   a. **What**: Utilize the insights gained from the analysis to guide continuous improvement efforts, making necessary adjustments to policies, procedures, and controls.
   b. **Who**: School leadership, IT experts, and other relevant experts.

6. **Manage Non-Conformities and Undesirable Trends**
   a. **What**: Establish procedures for acting on any non-conformities or undesirable trends observed, including root cause analysis, corrective actions, and preventive measures.

    b. **Who**: Risk management team, IT department, and school administrators.

7. **Document the Monitoring Process**
   a. **What**: Maintain comprehensive documentation of the monitoring process, including what resources are responsible for collecting the data, analysing the data, and acting on findings.
   b. **Who**: Compliance officers, risk management team, and IT staff.

8. **Review and Update Regularly**
   a. **What**: Regularly review and update the monitoring framework to ensure that it remains aligned with the school's evolving needs, technology, regulations, etc.
   b. **Who**: Ongoing responsibility of the ISMS management team, with periodic external audits if necessary.

Monitoring and measuring the ISMS is a continuous and collaborative process that requires careful planning, execution, and oversight. In the context of high schools, it involves aligning with both the specific needs of the educational environment and the requirements of standards like ISO 27001. By defining clear KPIs, implementing regular data collection and analysis, guiding continuous improvement, and maintaining transparent documentation, schools can ensure that their ISMS remains robust, responsive, and resilient. This not only enhances the security posture but also fosters a culture of accountability and excellence, reflecting the school's commitment to safeguarding its community's information and trust.

Building for continual improvement

A commitment to continual improvement is a core requirement of ISO 27001. Chapter 6 goes into further detail regarding the different mechanisms engaged for monitoring, maintaining, and improving the ISMS.

Documenting the ISMS

The ISMS needs to be documented in a comprehensive manner as per the both the standard's requirements and those of the school, stored securely and be available to those who need it. Furthermore, the documentation asset needs to be managed for updating including version control and records of authors and reviewers.

Summary

By developing robust information security policies, implementing effective security controls, conducting risk assessments, enacting risk treatment plans, and establishing a framework for monitoring and continual improvement, schools can build a strong ISMS that meets the requirements of ISO 27001 and helps protect their information assets.

ONGOING MAINTENANCE AND IMPROVEMENT OF THE ISMS

Chapter 6: Ongoing Maintenance and Improvement of the ISMS

Continual improvement

As discussed at the end of Chapter 5, it is essential to ISO 27001 to ensure the school has a process for continual improvement of the ISMS.

Develop a plan for identifying opportunities for improvement, incorporating feedback from internal audits, risk assessments, monitoring activities, management reviews, and stakeholder input. Implement improvements in a timely manner and ensure that their impact on the ISMS is evaluated and documented.

Tools used for ongoing maintenance and improvement.

We have already covered Risk Assessment and Risk Treatment Plans in Chapter 5. These form an important role in addressing areas where the ISMS may no longer be meeting an acceptable level of risk.

Also discussed in Chapter 5 was having appropriate monitoring built into the ISMS. This provides insight into the regular operation of the ISMS and means that issues can be detected and addressed in a timely manner. This requires clear procedures, roles and responsibilities regarding how the data is collected and analysed and how non-compliances or anomalies are addressed.

We will now look at two further inclusions required by ISO 27001 that assist with checking that the ISMS is meeting school and ISO 27001 requirements.

Management Reviews and Internal Audits.

Management reviews

Periodic management reviews are essential for evaluating the performance of the ISMS, making sure it is still meeting the school's information security requirements and risk appetite, and maintaining executive support. Schedule management reviews at least annually, involving key decision-makers from the executive team and governing body. During the review, present the results of internal audits, risk assessments, and performance monitoring activities, highlighting successes, challenges, and opportunities for improvement. Ensure that decisions and actions arising from management reviews are documented and implemented in a timely manner.

Conducting internal audits

Regular internal audits are crucial for ensuring compliance with ISO 27001 and identifying areas for improvement. Develop an internal audit plan that covers all aspects of the ISMS, including policies, procedures, controls, and risk management processes. Train internal auditors or engage external consultants to conduct audits, ensuring that they have the necessary knowledge and experience. If internal resources are used, it is important to ensure that there is no conflict of interest and that they do not feel pressure from other internal parties to overlook shortcomings. Varying the auditors can give more comprehensive outcomes. Document audit findings, share them with relevant stakeholders, and develop an action plan to address any identified gaps or weaknesses.

Summary

There are several elements that must be applied to the ISMS for checking function and managing ongoing improvements to meet ISO 27001 requirements. The key ones mentioned here are Risk Assessments, Risk Treatment Plans, Monitoring and analysing the data collected, Management Reviews and Internal Audits. All these tools serve to continually check that the ISMS is performing as required by both the school and the ISO 27001 standard and they provide the opportunities to identify areas for improvement so that the ISMS can serve the school community better year in, year out.

LET'S MAKE A DIFFERENCE!

ENGAGING AND TRAINING THE SCHOOL COMMUNITY

Chapter 7: Engaging and Training the School Community

Creating a security-aware culture

A security-aware culture is essential for the successful implementation and maintenance of an ISMS. Encourage a sense of shared responsibility for information security among all members of the school community, including staff, students, and parents. Foster a learning environment that supports the development of security awareness and skills and recognize the achievements and contributions of individuals and teams in promoting a secure environment.

Training and awareness programs for staff

School staff naturally have access to sensitive information. While some security controls may be technical, it is likely that, for usability of school information systems, many controls that relate to staff handling of data assets will be procedural controls. It is important that staff are competent when following the necessary procedures that relate to the ISMS and have an awareness of the importance of data security.

Develop targeted training and awareness programs for staff, that are strongly supported by school management, addressing their specific roles and responsibilities within the ISMS. Topics may include data protection, secure communication, incident reporting, and risk management. Offer training in various formats, such as workshops, e-learning modules, and interactive exercises, to accommodate different learning preferences and schedules. Regularly update and refresh training content to ensure that it remains relevant and engaging.

It is important for school management to provide positive messaging about staff training and awareness as it relates to the ISMS and promote the idea of it being a shared responsibility. Competence in this area should be included in staff performance measures.

Engaging students in information security

Incorporate information security education into the school curriculum, teaching students about the importance of protecting their personal information and using technology responsibly. Offer age-appropriate lessons and activities that engage students in learning about topics such as cybersecurity, data privacy, and online safety. Encourage students to take an active role in promoting a secure learning environment, by participating in initiatives such as peer mentoring programs, cybersecurity clubs, and awareness campaigns.

Involving parents and guardians

Parents and guardians play a critical role in supporting the school's commitment to information security. Keep them informed about the school's ISMS and the steps being taken to protect sensitive information. Offer resources and guidance on how they can support their children's understanding of information security and safe online practices. Encourage open communication and feedback from parents and guardians and address any concerns or questions they may have.

Continuous improvement of training and engagement efforts

Regularly evaluate the effectiveness of training and engagement efforts, using feedback from staff, students, and parents, as well as performance data and other indicators. Identify areas for improvement and update training content and engagement strategies as needed. Stay informed about the latest trends and best practices in information security education, and continually seek opportunities to enhance the school community's knowledge and skills.

Summary

By engaging and training the school community in information security, schools can foster a security-aware culture that supports the successful implementation and maintenance of an ISMS and contributes to a safer and more secure learning environment. Furthermore, it is essential for school staff to understand and embrace their roles in the ISMS. Training and awareness initiatives are key ways to obtain this engagement.

Preparing for Certification

Chapter 8: Preparing for Certification

Preparing for the certification audit

Thorough preparation helps ensure a successful ISO 27001 certification process.

Once the ISMS has been established, with all security controls, required policy, process, roles and documentation in place, and all action items identified in the treatment plan addressed, the best way to check your preparedness is by conducting an internal audit as described in Chapter 6.

Ensure your internal audit covers all areas of the ISMS as defined in ISO 27001 and is performed in an unbiased manner so it reflects the likely outcome of the certification audit. Review the results of the internal audit as well as any management reviews and risk treatment plans, confirming that all identified gaps or weaknesses have been addressed.

Prepare and check necessary documentation, such as policies, procedures, risk assessments, and records of training and awareness programs.

As the ISO 27001 certification process approaches, ensure that the school community is well-prepared for the external audit. Engage staff, students, and in the process, ensuring that they are familiar with the ISMS and ready to demonstrate their commitment to information security.

Selecting a certification body

Selecting a certification body for ISO 27001 is a crucial step in the certification process, and it requires careful consideration and due diligence. Begin by identifying certification bodies that are accredited by recognized national or international accreditation bodies, as this ensures that they comply with relevant standards and regulations. Evaluate the certification bodies based on their experience, expertise in your specific industry or sector, and their reputation in the market. Request references and speak with previous clients to gauge their satisfaction and the effectiveness of the certification body's approach. Consider the cost, but also look at the value they provide, such as additional support, guidance, or post-certification services. Finally, ensure that the certification body understands the unique needs and context of your organization, such as in the case of a high school, where specific considerations around student data and educational regulations may apply. The selection should be a collaborative decision involving key stakeholders, aligning with the organization's goals, budget, and risk management strategy.

What to expect from the certification audit

An ISO 27001 certification audit is a systematic examination of an organization's Information Security Management System (ISMS) to verify compliance with the ISO 27001 standard. It's a critical milestone in achieving certification and demonstrates a commitment to information security. Here's what to expect from this process:

1. **Preparation Phase**
    a. **Internal Audit**: Before the external audit, conduct an internal audit to identify potential gaps and areas for improvement.
    b. **Documentation Review**: Ensure that all required documentation, such as policies, procedures, risk assessments, and risk treatment plans, is in place and up to date.

    c. **Selecting a Certification Body**: Choose an accredited certification body that fits your organization's needs and industry.

2. **Stage 1: Readiness Review**
   a. **Initial Assessment**: The auditor reviews the ISMS documentation to ensure that it meets the standard's requirements.
   b. **Site Visit**: The auditor may visit the premises to understand the organizational context and scope of the ISMS.
   c. **Feedback and Planning**: Receive feedback on any non-conformities and plan for the Stage 2 audit.

3. **Stage 2: Compliance Audit**
   a. **Detailed Examination**: The auditor conducts a thorough examination of the ISMS, including interviews, observations, and document reviews.
   b. **Compliance Check**: The focus is on verifying that the ISMS is implemented and maintained according to the ISO 27001 requirements.
   c. **Non-Conformity Identification**: If any non-conformities are identified, the organization must address them within a specified timeframe.

4. **Certification Decision**
   a. **Review of Findings**: The certification body reviews the audit findings and any corrective actions taken.
   b. **Certification Grant:** If the organization meets all requirements, the certification body grants ISO 27001 certification.

    c. **Certification Document**: Receive the official certification document, valid for three years, subject to surveillance audits.

5. **Post-Certification Activities**
   a. **Surveillance Audits**: Regular surveillance audits are conducted to ensure ongoing compliance with the standard.
   b. **Continuous Improvement**: Use the insights gained from the audit to drive continuous improvement in the ISMS.

6. **Potential Challenges and Considerations**
   a. **Resource Allocation**: Ensure that adequate resources, including time and personnel, are allocated for the audit process.
   b. **Stakeholder Engagement**: Engage relevant stakeholders, such as IT staff, management, and external experts if needed.
   c. **Confidentiality and Integrity**: Ensure that the audit process maintains the confidentiality and integrity of sensitive information.

An ISO 27001 certification audit is a rigorous and comprehensive process that requires careful preparation, active participation, and a commitment to continuous improvement. It's an opportunity to validate the effectiveness of the ISMS, identify areas for enhancement, and demonstrate compliance with a globally recognized standard. By understanding what to expect and actively engaging in the process, organizations can navigate the audit with confidence and leverage it as a valuable tool for strengthening their information security posture.

Maintaining ISO 27001 certification

Once the school has achieved ISO 27001 certification, it is essential to maintain compliance with the standard and continue to improve the ISMS. Regularly review and update policies, procedures, and controls to reflect changes in the school's environment, risk landscape, and the standard itself.

Continue to conduct internal audits, management reviews, and risk assessments, using the results to direct corrective action where necessary and to guide ongoing improvement efforts. Communicate the school's ongoing commitment to information security to stakeholders and celebrate the achievements and milestones of the ISMS.

Summary

There are a lot of requirements in the ISO 27001 standard that need to be met for successful certification. It is helpful for the school to check their preparedness by doing an internal audit and checking that all required actions from earlier risk treatment plans or management reviews have been addressed. Achieving certification legitimizes the efforts taken to protect the school's data.

Furthermore, by maintaining certification and continuously improving the ISMS, schools can demonstrate their long-term commitment to information security and the protection of their community's sensitive information.

ISO 27001 CERTIFICATION IN SCHOOLS

LESSONS LEARNED AND BEST PRACTICES

Chapter 9: Lessons Learned and Best Practices for ISO 27001 Certification in Schools

Engage stakeholders early

To ensure a successful ISO 27001 certification process, it is essential to engage stakeholders from the outset. Include representatives from various departments, such as IT, administration, and teaching staff, in the planning and implementation process. This will help garner support and foster a sense of shared ownership over the ISMS.

Develop a realistic timeline

Implementing an ISMS and achieving ISO 27001 certification can be a complex and time-consuming process. Develop a realistic timeline that includes milestones and deadlines for key tasks, considering the resources available and potential challenges. Regularly review and update the timeline as needed and communicate progress to stakeholders.

Allocate sufficient resources

Ensure that adequate resources, including budget, personnel, and technology, are allocated to the ISO 27001 certification project. This will help ensure a smooth implementation process and reduce the likelihood of delays or setbacks.

Foster a security-aware culture

A strong security-aware culture is essential for the successful implementation and maintenance of an ISMS. Develop training and awareness programs tailored to the needs of different stakeholder groups, emphasizing the role that each individual plays in protecting the school's information assets. Regularly share updates on the progress of the ISO 27001 certification process, celebrate milestones, and acknowledge the contributions of individuals and teams in fostering a secure environment.

Learn from others

Collaborate with other schools and organizations that have achieved ISO 27001 certification, learning from their experiences and best practices. This can provide valuable insights and guidance for your own certification journey and help identify potential challenges and solutions.

Continuous improvement

Embrace the principle of continuous improvement, regularly reviewing and updating the ISMS to ensure it remains effective and compliant with ISO 27001 requirements. Use feedback from internal audits, management reviews, and stakeholder input to identify areas for improvement, and implement changes in a timely manner.

Summary

By following these lessons learned and best practices, schools can increase their chances of a successful ISO 27001 certification process and enjoy the benefits of a robust and effective information security management system.

CONCLUSION

Conclusion
The long-term benefits of ISO 27001 certification

The long-term benefits of ISO 27001 certification extend beyond the immediate achievement of meeting the standard's requirements. These benefits can have a lasting impact on a school's information security, reputation, and overall success. Some of the key long-term benefits include:

1. **Enhanced information security**: ISO 27001 certification demonstrates that a school has implemented a robust and comprehensive Information Security Management System (ISMS) that effectively addresses potential risks to its information assets. Over time, this leads to a more secure environment for sensitive data, ensuring that the confidentiality, integrity, and availability of information are maintained.

2. **Improved risk management**: The ISO 27001 framework emphasizes proactive risk management, which helps schools identify and address potential threats before they become critical issues. This focus on risk management ensures that schools continuously evaluate and improve their security posture, staying ahead of emerging threats and vulnerabilities.

3. **Increased stakeholder confidence**: By achieving ISO 27001 certification, schools can demonstrate their commitment to information security to students, parents, staff, and other stakeholders. This builds trust and confidence in the school's ability to safeguard sensitive data and maintain a secure learning environment.

4. **Enhanced reputation and competitiveness**: ISO 27001 certification can serve as a competitive advantage for schools, setting them apart from institutions that have not achieved this level of information security maturity. This can lead to increased enrolment, partnerships, and overall recognition in the education sector.

5. **Greater operational efficiency**: Implementing an ISMS in accordance with ISO 27001 often leads to more efficient and streamlined processes, as schools must evaluate and optimize their information security practices. This can result in cost savings, reduced duplication of efforts, and improved resource allocation.

6. **Legal and regulatory compliance**: ISO 27001 certification helps schools comply with legal and regulatory requirements related to information security and data protection, such as the General Data Protection Regulation (GDPR). This reduces the risk of fines, penalties, and reputational damage associated with non-compliance.

7. **Continual improvement**: The ISO 27001 standard emphasizes the importance of continuous improvement, ensuring that schools regularly review and enhance their information security practices. This ongoing commitment to improvement helps institutions stay current with best practices and adapt to the changing threat landscape.

8. **Employee awareness and engagement**: A crucial aspect of ISO 27001 certification is the development of security awareness programs and

training for staff and students. This not only raises the overall security knowledge within the school but also fosters a security-aware culture that supports the long-term success of the ISMS.

Overall, the long-term benefits of ISO 27001 certification make it a worthwhile investment for schools looking to demonstrate their commitment to information security, protect their sensitive data, and maintain a secure learning environment.

The importance of a secure educational environment for future generations

A secure educational environment is vital for the development and well-being of future generations. It not only ensures the safety and privacy of students, staff, and parents, but also creates a stable foundation for learning and personal growth. Here are some key reasons why a secure educational environment is essential for future generations:

1. **Protecting personal and sensitive information**: Schools collect, store, and process vast amounts of sensitive information, including personal data about students, staff, and families. A secure educational environment safeguards this information from unauthorized access, disclosure, or misuse, ensuring privacy and maintaining trust between the school and its community.
2. **Fostering a safe learning environment**: A secure educational environment helps protect students and staff from cyber threats, such as malware, phishing, and online harassment. This creates a safer digital space for students to learn,

explore, and engage with technology without fear of potential harm.

3. **Encouraging responsible digital citizenship**: By promoting a secure educational environment, schools can teach students the importance of responsible digital citizenship. This includes understanding the risks and responsibilities associated with using technology and sharing personal information online, as well as developing skills to protect themselves and others in the digital world.

4. **Building trust and confidence**: A secure educational environment builds trust and confidence among students, staff, and parents. It demonstrates the school's commitment to protecting sensitive information and providing a safe space for learning, which can enhance the school's reputation and strengthen community bonds.

5. **Supporting academic success**: A secure educational environment allows students and staff to focus on learning and teaching, without the distractions and disruptions caused by security breaches or cyber threats. This contributes to an atmosphere conducive to academic success, helping students reach their full potential.

6. **Complying with legal and regulatory requirements**: Schools are subject to various legal and regulatory requirements related to information security and data protection. By ensuring a secure educational environment, schools can comply with these requirements and avoid potential penalties, fines, or reputational damage.

7. **Preparing students for future careers**: As technology continues to play an increasingly significant role in our lives, the demand for individuals with strong cybersecurity skills will grow. A secure educational environment helps students develop the necessary skills and knowledge to pursue careers in this field, contributing to a more secure and resilient digital landscape for future generations.

8. **Promoting innovation and collaboration**: A secure educational environment enables students and staff to experiment with new technologies, collaborate on projects, and explore innovative ideas without fear of compromising their privacy or security. This fosters a culture of creativity and innovation that can drive future advancements in education and beyond.

In summary, a secure educational environment is crucial for the well-being and development of future generations, as it helps protect sensitive information, fosters safe learning experiences, and prepares students to navigate the digital world responsibly and confidently.

ISO 27001 Controls

ISO 27001 Controls

ISO 27001 controls are held in Annex A and are listed below:

Section	Control
5.1	Policies for information security
5.2	Information security roles and responsibilities
5.3	Segregation of duties
5.4	Management responsibilities
5.5	Contact with authorities
5.6	Contact with special interest groups
5.7	Threat intelligence
5.8	Information security in project management
5.9	Inventory of information and other associated assets
5.10	Acceptable use of information and other associated assets
5.11	Return of assets
5.12	Classification of information
5.13	Labelling of information
5.14	Information transfer
5.15	Access control
5.16	Identity management
5.17	Authentication information
5.18	Access rights
5.19	Information security in supplier relationships
5.20	Addressing information security within supplier agreements
5.21	Managing information security in the ICT supply chain
5.22	Monitoring, review and change management of supplier services
5.23	Information security for use of cloud services

Section	Control
5.24	Information security incident management planning and preparation
5.25	Assessment and decision on information security events
5.26	Response to information security incidents
5.27	Learning from information security incidents
5.28	Collection of evidence
5.29	Information security during disruption
5.30	ICT readiness for business continuity
5.31	Legal, statutory, regulatory and contractual requirements
5.32	Intellectual property rights
5.33	Protection of records
5.34	Privacy and protection of personal identifiable information (PII)
5.35	Independent review of information security
5.36	Compliance with policies, rules and standards for information security
5.37	Documented operating procedures
6.1	Screening
6.2	Terms and conditions of employment
6.3	Information security awareness, education and training
6.4	Disciplinary process
6.5	Responsibilities after termination or change of employment
6.6	Confidentiality or non-disclosure agreements
6.7	Remote working
6.8	Information security event reporting
7.1	Physical security perimeters
7.2	Physical entry
7.3	Securing offices, rooms and facilities
7.4	Physical security monitoring
7.5	Protecting against physical and environmental threats

Section	Control
7.6	Working in secure areas
7.7	Clear desk and clear screen
7.8	Equipment siting and protection
7.9	Security of assets off-premises
7.10	Storage media
7.11	Supporting utilities
7.12	Cabling security
7.13	Equipment maintenance
7.14	Secure disposal or re-use of equipment
8.1	User end point devices
8.2	Privileged access rights
8.3	Information access restriction
8.4	Access to source code
8.5	Secure authentication
8.6	Capacity management
8.7	Protection against malware
8.8	Management of technical vulnerabilities
8.9	Configuration management
8.10	Information deletion
8.11	Data masking
8.12	Data leakage prevention
8.13	Information backup
8.14	Redundancy of information processing facilities
8.15	Logging
8.16	Monitoring activities
8.17	Clock synchronization
8.18	Use of privileged utility programs
8.19	Installation of software on operational systems
8.20	Networks security
8.21	Security of network services
8.22	Segregation of networks
8.23	Web filtering
8.24	Use of cryptography

Section	Control
8.25	Secure development life cycle
8.26	Application security requirements
8.27	Secure system architecture and engineering principles
8.28	Secure coding
8.29	Security testing in development and acceptance
8.30	Outsourced development
8.31	Separation of development, test and production environments
8.32	Change management
8.33	Test information
8.34	Protection of information systems during audit testing

Getting Help

It's perfectly reasonable to work on implementing ISO 27001 for your school internally or with external engagement. To make this even easier for you, we've developed a guided service which helps you develop all the required policies, documents and processes to help you achieve certification.

Take a look at www.isoforschools.com for more information on how to achieve ISO 27001 certification at speed and with amazing quality.

www.ingramcontent.com/pod-product-compliance
Lightning Source LLC
LaVergne TN
LVHW072049060326
832903LV00053B/311